D0371871

Management Tips

Management Tips
From Harvard Business Review

Harvard Business Review Press

Boston, Massachusetts

Library of Congress Cataloging-in-Publication Data

Management tips / by Harvard business review.
    p. cm.
  ISBN 978-1-4221-5878-4 (alk. paper)
1. Management. 2. Leadership. 3. Organizational change.
I. Harvard business review.
  HD31.M293893 2011
  658—dc22

                                         2011016547

The paper used in this publication meets the requirements of
the American National Standard for Permanence of Paper
for Publications and Documents in Libraries and Archives
Z39.48-1992.

Contents

About the Book   vii

Managing Yourself   1

Managing Your Team   67

Managing Your Business   129

Attributions   195

Index   207

About the Book

Management Tips is a compilation of the Management Tip of the Day by *Harvard Business Review*. Adapted from blog posts and other content, these tips offer quick and practical advice on how to manage yourself, manage your team, and manage your business. Please turn to the List of Attributions at the back of the book for more information on the sources from which these tips were adapted, and visit hbr.org for more tips and content.

Managing Yourself

01

Create a New Leadership Vision

Now is the time to clarify and refine your leadership vision. This requires both articulating your values and reexamining your goals for the future.

Start by identifying the four or five most important episodes in your life—moments that defined who you are today. For each episode, articulate how it shaped your values.

Then draft a statement of your personal leadership vision. This is a compelling image of an achievable future. Describe the kind of leader you want to become and the major contributions you want to make to the world between now and 2025. What will you be doing in 2025, and what impact do you hope to be making?

02

Pretend You Have What You Want

Your mind is often your greatest tool, but as anyone who has been taken over by fear, frustration, or worry knows, it can also be your greatest enemy. Whether you're concerned that you don't have the respect of your peers or that a customer isn't calling you back because she's gone to a competitor, overthinking the issue only serves to compound the worry. Instead, pretend you have what you want. Act as if your peers respect you or as if the customer is loyal. These may be fantasies, but what you're worrying about may be as well. It's better to stop the worry and act confidently; chances are better that you'll get what you want.

Take Ownership

Autonomy, influence, and a sense of meaning are all associated with lower stress. If you need to find more joy, take on a new project that will improve your job, team, or workplace. While you may not have the same degree of freedom that an entrepreneur does, you can find ways to set the agenda and claim ownership of tasks and projects. This ownership will likely improve your job satisfaction while adding an important accomplishment to your résumé.

04

Take Responsibility for Your Growth

Responsibility for your professional development lies squarely on your shoulders. No matter your situation, use these tips to keep sharp:

- *Meet with two former coworkers each month.* Talk about your industry and where it is headed. This will keep you tapped into the community.
- *Have one major learning experience each quarter.* If your work isn't giving you the necessary challenges, seek out other opportunities. Volunteer for a nonprofit, attend a conference, or take a class.
- *Give yourself a performance review.* Reflect on your growth and performance, whether through a formal process or not. Be honest with yourself about your strengths and weaknesses and what you should focus on in the coming year.

Increase Your Desire to Learn

Don't let your ego get in the way of your desire to learn. Successful leaders keep their minds open to new things because they know that no matter how high their level of mastery, there is always more to discover. If you've become an expert in one field, seek out other fields where you can transfer and apply your expertise. When facing challenges, even ones you've faced many times before, adopt a learner's approach—ask questions or find new ways to solve the problem.

Give Yourself a Leadership Workup

Many of us wait until we're sick to see a doctor. However, preventive medical assessments have been shown to improve health, save lives, and reduce medical costs. Prevention can be beneficial to leadership assessments too. Often people are asked to see a coach or participate in a 360-degree assessment when troubles surface. Yet, time and money (not to mention headaches) could be saved if leaders underwent thorough assessments before problems arose. Ask the people around you for feedback about what's working and what's not. Be sure you understand their expectations and where you may not be meeting them, or are unnecessarily exceeding them. Having a complete understanding of where you are as a leader gives you a greater sense of control and power to shape your future.

07

Work on Your Backhand

When you're particularly good at something, it's easy to rely on that strength. For example, if your forehand is your stronger stroke, you'll position yourself to use it much more often. But turning weaknesses into strengths will give you a competitive edge and make you a more effective leader. Focus energy on improving your weak points. Think about your last performance review or ask your peers what one capability you really need to succeed in the current environment. There's no better way to impress than to reveal a killer backhand when everyone's expecting your forehand.

08

Shed Your Excessive Need to Be You

One of the worst habits a leader can have is excusing his behavior with claims like, "That's just the way I am!" Stop clinging to bad behaviors because you believe they are essential to who you are. Instead of insisting that you can't change, think about how these behaviors may be impeding the success of those around you. Don't think of these behaviors as character traits, but as possibilities for improvement. You'll be surprised how easily you can change when it helps you succeed.

Be Open to Criticism

Constructive criticism is essential for creativity, innovation, and problem solving. Since leadership requires all three, leaders need to be sure not only that they are open to criticism, but that they actively seek it out. Don't simply ask for general feedback but ask people—direct reports, peers, customers—to poke holes in your ideas and approaches. Critique can be a useful approach to test ideas and keep people and teams accountable.

Listen Better

For years, leadership experts have been encouraging managers to improve their listening skills. Good listening isn't just about making the speaker feel respected and heard; it's also about making sure you understand what's truly said. Here are three tips for better listening:

- *Think.* Engage in the conversation by thinking ahead and anticipating what the speaker is going to say. Try to anticipate the conclusions. Don't just hear the words.
- *Review.* Pause briefly and mentally summarize the points.
- *Listen.* Watch nonverbal cues that could indicate what the speaker isn't saying. What isn't said is often as important as what is.

Schedule Regular Meetings with Yourself

As we continue venturing into uncharted economic waters, how can you keep your job on track and deliver your best? Schedule a weekly meeting with yourself. That's right: no matter how busy you are, this is not a luxury. It's essential.

Every week, take a quiet hour to reflect on recent critical events—conflicts, failures, opportunities you exploited, observations of others' behavior, feedback from others. Consider how you responded, what went well, what didn't, and what might be more effective in the future.

Never cancel this meeting—it's crucial.

12

Managing Your Energy

As organizations demand more and more from their people, time-pressed employees have to scramble to keep up. You may not be able to make the day any longer, but you can replenish your energy. Use these four simple ways to help you work smarter and prevent burnout:

- *Take brief but regular breaks.* Step away from your desk every 90 to 120 minutes. Take a walk, get a drink, or just stretch your legs.
- *Say thank you.* Being positive boosts your energy level. Regularly express appreciation to others.
- *Reduce interruptions.* Perform tasks that need concentration away from phones and e-mail. Instead, designate specific times in your day to respond to messages.

- *Do what you love.* Understand where your strengths lie and what you enjoy doing. Find ways to do more of those things and less of what tires you out.

13

Decrease Your Technology Dependence

How often do you hear someone ask, "What did we do before cellphones?" One of the many answers is: we relied on our memories. Studies have shown that using our memories improves reasoning and creativity. Yet, because of our increased reliance on technology, few of us can even recall phone numbers or appointments. Try remembering and entering numbers by hand or picturing your weekly calendar in your mind. This will not only help you use your mind in a healthy way, but may save you when the inevitable happens and your BlackBerry or iPhone goes down.

Capture Big Ideas in Simple Ways

Don't rely on your memory or BlackBerry to record and capitalize on good ideas. Go old-school with a stack of 3 x 5 index cards. Carry them with you and, when you hear a good idea, write it down. The physicality of the cards forces you to reflect on them at the end of the day, and the act of writing down the ideas helps you remember and process them. Having the blank cards in your pocket is also a useful reminder to be looking for new ideas and, most importantly, to listen.

15

Combine Creativity and Results

In academia, critical thinking is the norm, and asking questions is required. On most campuses, questioning ideas is the first step, and the second is questioning the question. As a result, academia has a reputation for being too open-ended and sluggish. In industry, we prefer to set a deadline, get things done, focus on execution. We worry that thinking about an idea could hold up progress. Combine the two approaches to be sure you are both thinking creatively and getting results. Ask lots of questions but don't let the questions impede movement. The questions should drive you toward a clear, defensible outcome.

16

Get Creative by Zoning Out

Studies have shown that an idle brain is more likely to come up with a new idea. Yet, we often feel that we need more focus. Try taking mental breaks from e-mail and deadlines and let your mind wander. These breaks can be critical to remaining creative and open to fresh ideas. You can take a short break during a hectic day or you can opt for a longer, creative sabbatical over a week, month, or year. Regardless of the duration, be sure you are giving your mind needed space to think for the long term and big picture.

17

Make Masterful Decisions

Whether you believe in making decisions swiftly and decisively or with more caution and deliberation, try these three tips to help you reach better conclusions and avoid decision traps:

- *Get the right minds on the job.* Decision making is the process of converting input into output. To make the best decision, optimize your input by getting the opinions and insights of trusted people who know the arena best.
- *Decide how you will decide.* Bickering often happens during the decision-making process. Be clear with yourself and others involved about the steps you will take to reach the decision.

- *Demand diversity.* Too much agreement is dangerous; you need dissenting opinions. Give a minority viewpoint a voice or appoint a devil's advocate. Listening to the "other side" will give you a more robust answer.

18

Trust in Your Decision-Making Skills

Yes, knowledge is power, but too much knowledge can take away your power. When solving problems, many leaders gather an abundance of information and conduct in-depth analyses to give them what they hope are the right answers. This can lead to analysis paralysis or to data-driven, but illogical, answers. Often the best answers are educated guesses informed by your past experiences coupled with new information and insight. Don't put too much faith in information analysis alone, and don't disregard your decision-making skills. Remember to always check answers with your gut feelings before acting.

Find Extra Time

Crises and special events force us to find extra time in our day for crucial tasks. In an ordinary week, however, those hours are buried in unnecessary meetings, interruptions, and inefficiency. Don't wait for the next emergency. Here are two ways to regain wasted time:

- *Analyze your calendar.* Look back at the last month. Which meetings were truly needed to advance your goals? Then look forward at the coming month and eliminate ones that you can bypass without any consequence.

- *Ask for feedback.* Our worst time-wasting activities are often invisible to us. Ask direct reports and peers to identify tasks that you could do less often or stop altogether.

20

Manage with Minimum Time

Do you strive to be a good manager or mentor, but feel you do not have the time to do it well? Don't get trapped into thinking that leadership is an extra commitment on top of your day job. How you lead, not how much, is what counts. Here are three ways to maximize your management in minimum time:

- *Turn dead time into development time.* Look for every small stretch in your day when you could be talking to someone and convert each into a coaching opportunity. Walking out of a meeting? Use those two minutes to give your direct report feedback on the presentation.

- *Show up in people's work spaces.* Once per day, get up and walk over to the desk of someone you haven't spoken to recently.

Take two minutes to ask her what she's working on.

- *Make two contacts per day.* Every day, e-mail two people you met with that day and offer "feedforward." Employees who know that you're trying to develop their skills will stay engaged.

21

Increase Your Productivity

We live in a demanding and distracting world. Being productive can sometimes feel like an impossible feat. Here are three ways to get more done without burning out:

- *Keep one to-do list.* Include everything you want or need to do in one place. Writing it down helps get it off your mind and leaves you free to focus on the task at hand.

- *Do the most important thing first.* Before you leave work in the evening, decide what one thing you need to accomplish the next day. Do it first thing in the morning, when you're likely to have the most energy and fewest distractions.

- *Schedule time for non-urgent things.* It's easy to get caught up in the pressing issues of the day. Block off time in your calendar to do things that would otherwise get squeezed out, like writing, thinking creatively, or building relationships.

22

Get Through Your To-Do List

Self-discipline is hard. Try these three tips to make your work more efficient every day:

- *Get three things done before noon.* Statistics show that the team ahead at halftime is more likely to win the game. Enjoy your lunch knowing that you accomplished at least three tasks in the morning.

- *Sequence for speed.* Break projects into parts. Take on the longer pieces at the beginning and make sure each subsequent part is shorter. If you leave the longest parts for last, you are more likely to run out of steam before the end of the day.

- *Tackle similar tasks at the same time.* The mind thrives on repetition. You can build momentum by taking on similar projects at the same time.

Prioritize Value over Volume

Research has shown that multitasking results in mediocre outcomes. By putting too little attention on too many things, you fail to do anything well. However, the answer isn't single-tasking either. Single-tasking is far too slow to help you succeed in today's fast-paced world. Instead, identify the tasks that will create the most value and focus on those. By prioritizing value over volume and sharpening your focus on tasks that truly matter, you'll increase the quality of your work and, ultimately, the value you provide. What to do with all those tasks that didn't make the high-value list? Put them on a "do later" list. If they continually fail to make it to the high-value list, ask yourself: why do them at all?

24

Develop a Growth Mind-set

We spend a lot of time and energy at work trying not to fail. However, most people describe their failures as an important part of learning and growing. Adapt a growth mind-set and accept that failure is part of the process of skill development. People with a growth mind-set feel smart when they're learning, not just when they're succeeding. Don't limit yourself to doing things that you know you can do—you won't grow that way. Instead, try things that are above your ability and set high goals that you aren't sure you can reach. You might surprise yourself and succeed, and if you don't, you'll learn something new.

Achieve Short-Term Goals

Development efforts often focus on how you can achieve your career goals over the long term. Short-term successes, however, are critical to making your next move and preparing for those long-term aspirations. Here are three immediate ways to build your career options:

- *Play to your strengths.* Do more of what you do best. Early in a career, it makes sense to try a bit of everything and push to improve in areas of weakness, but at a certain point, it is better to focus on your strengths.

- *Reinforce your "brand."* Choose activities outside work that develop the image you want to convey. For example, volunteer for the school building committee if you're good at managing projects. Gain broader experience and conversational ways to reinforce your capabilities at work.

- *Create the context for success.* Surround yourself with people you need to do your work well. People have to recognize common values and goals before they're likely to share what they know, so invest in these relationships.

Give Up Control

Leaders who micromanage do a disservice to their company, their employees, and themselves; worse yet, they are often preventing their companies from growing. If you are struggling to grow your company or unit, one of the smartest things you can do is give up control. Here's how:

- *Push down decision making.* If you're making all the decisions, you're only holding your company back. Push decision making down to the lowest possible level.
- *Accept that mistakes will happen.* Sharing responsibility with others means things don't always go according to plan. Prepare your employees to avoid mistakes by being clear about your expectations and giving them the tools they need to do their jobs well.

- ***Build your bench.*** Making yourself comfortable with giving up control requires having people you believe in. Invest both your time and resources to develop your star employees.

Avoid Micromanaging Yourself

Training yourself to avoid micromanaging others is one thing, but handling tendencies to control your own work can be even harder. Here are three ways to keep the micromanager in you from impeding your work:

- *Keep your eyes on the prize.* Don't focus on details before the big picture is laid out. Keep the larger project goal in mind and resist temptation to dive into minutiae.
- *Don't second-guess yourself.* You'll inconvenience yourself and the people who work for you if you shift project direction midstream. Take a complete pass through a project before deciding to change course.

- *Micromanage when it's time.* Almost every project requires some detail work. When you reach that point, unleash the micromanager in you and handle it.

How to Beat Burnout

Falling prey to burnout is easy. This condition—marked by exhaustion, cynicism, and inefficacy—stems from information overload, perpetual "busyness," and a relentless race against the clock.

One tactic for preventing burnout is to seek out ways to use available resources more wisely. For instance, delegate responsibilities to staff members eager to develop new skills. And resist the urge to grapple with urgent but unimportant tasks (such as responding to e-mails). Instead, schedule set times during the day for checking and replying to e-mails and phone calls.

Manage Stress by Facing It

We've been told over and over about the harmful effects of stress, but how can we handle stress if its source doesn't go away? Figure out what your reaction to stress is. If you respond to stress by doing something productive—like cleaning your house or checking in more frequently with your team—consider yourself lucky. In the more likely case that your stress reaction is unhealthy, take notice. Some common reactions to stress are micromanaging, making heavy-handed suggestions, and second-guessing decisions. If you find yourself doing these things, pause and take a breath. Paying careful attention to your behavior can help you stop the reaction before it has harmful effects.

Stop Working and Have Fun

You don't have to retire early to stop working. You just need to take the "work" out of work. Make work fun by doing these two things:

- *Find people you enjoy working with.* Of course you don't always choose who you work with, but when you do, choose projects that allow you to work with people you trust, respect, and enjoy spending time with.

- *Find problems you enjoy solving.* Again, you may not always have a choice, but try to seek out projects you find interesting and are passionate about. If you're not excited about any of your current projects, propose a new project that you can lead.

31

Take a Mini Break

We all need a break. However, in the current environment, taking time off for a vacation may not be best for your company (or your bank account). Find ways to carve out smaller chunks of time to rest and recuperate. Here are three things you can do in one hour or less.

- *Exercise.* Make the time by trying an early morning class or exercising during your lunch break.

- *Turn off your BlackBerry.* Even for just an hour while you take a walk or have dinner with a friend, this "quiet" time will help you feel more focused when you power back on.

- *Do a crossword puzzle.* Research shows crossword puzzles sharpen the mind. Work on the puzzle while you eat lunch and give yourself a mental break.

32

Don't Let Strengths Be Weaknesses

Many of the qualities responsible for getting us where we are today can also hold us back. Watch out for these three double-edged traits:

- *Persistence.* Willingness to persevere despite obstacles has created many great innovations and is often the foundation for successful start-ups. However, persistence can easily turn to stubbornness. Stick with your ideas when you know you are right and have supporting evidence. Be willing to abandon your position when signs show you need help or redirection.

- *Control.* Early phases of company growth require the founder to be involved in all operations. But as the company scales, that maniacal attention to detail can be counterproductive. Recognize the importance of delegation and let go when it's time.

- *Loyalty.* Close ties inevitably form when people work together day in and out, and loyal relationships can yield great results. However, you need to know when loyalty is clouding your judgment in assessing capabilities and skill gaps.

Change Your Behavior

Developing yourself as a leader is not easy: behavioral change is hard, time consuming, and frustrating. However, removing the five most common roadblocks to change can make your path to self-improvement better:

- *Take ownership.* If you don't think you can change, you can't. Believe in your ability to change and take ownership before getting started.
- *Be patient.* Positive, lasting results take time, usually 50 percent to 100 percent longer than most people initially think.
- *Accept difficulties.* Real change takes real work. When setting out, be prepared to face challenges you didn't anticipate.
- *Refuse to be distracted.* Something more important will inevitably come up. You need to make your development

a priority and refuse to let distractions divert your path.

- *Maintain.* Once you've started to see traction, don't declare victory. Sustainable change requires maintenance over a lifetime.

Fire Yourself

Management shake-ups, though disruptive, can be good for a company. They bring in fresh perspectives and require that leaders take a hard look at their own performance. Do not wait for your company to get in trouble. Instead, fire yourself. Think about what you would do in your position if you were to start anew. What would you do differently if this were your first day on the job? Taking this step back can help you evaluate the strategies and approaches you are currently using, see things that are too difficult to see when you are entrenched, and reenergize yourself for the challenges ahead.

35

Cultivate Your Proactive Brain

Studies have shown that a good memory helps you better navigate the future. And in business, the ability to anticipate and negotiate future demands is an asset. A proactive brain uses details from past experiences to make analogies with your current surroundings. It then helps you determine where you are and envision future possibilities. We are all born with proactive brains, but these three things can help improve brain performance:

- *Give your brain a lot to work with.* Create a rich pool of information to draw from. Expose your brain to diverse experiences and situations.
- *Borrow from others.* Find out as much as you can about others' experiences by talking and interacting with people, and reading about their lives.

- *Let your mind wander.* Undisturbed time gives your brain the space it needs to recall and recombine past experiences in ways that help you anticipate the future.

Decipher and Achieve Success

Success in business is not about having the most brilliant answer. It's about having a workable solution, and that requires developing an understanding of the unwritten rules of the organization. To become more persuasive and effective, figure out who and what really matters. Ask successful people at your company what approaches and relationships helped them most. Be curious about the ways people get things done, and observe the inner workings of projects and initiatives you aren't part of by building relationships with influential people. All of the information you gather can contribute to your own future success.

Schedule Time for Second-Guessing

Questioning whether you have made the right decision can be a useful way to make sure you are on the right track. But if you second-guess yourself at the wrong time, you may feel tempted to give up on important commitments. Don't question yourself when you are most vulnerable. Instead, schedule a time to review your decision when you are in the right frame of mind. For example, don't wonder whether you should abandon a plan to talk more during meetings when you are walking into the conference room. Rather, tell yourself that you will question the decision ten minutes into the meeting, once you've had time to get used to the idea. Setting a time will also help you second-guess once rather than nagging yourself with doubts.

Be Confident, but Not Really Sure

One of the keys to effective decision making is confidence. Even if you only have temporary convictions, act on them. If you doubt your decision while making it, trust in your leadership may erode. Strong opinions signal confidence and provide others with the guidance they need. But resist the urge to cling to your decisions. Have the humility to realize that you might be wrong if better information comes along. And be prepared to change your mind and correct your course if that happens.

Recover from a Mistake

While most people accept that mistakes are inevitable, no one likes to make them. The good news is that even large slipups don't have to be career-enders if they are handled well. Next time you make a blunder, follow these three steps to recover gracefully:

- *Fess up.* Trying to hide a mistake or downplay its importance can be fatal to your career. Be candid and transparent about the mistake, take responsibility for your part in it, and don't be defensive.
- *Make necessary changes.* Mistakes are important learning opportunities. Explain to your boss and other interested parties what you will do differently going forward.
- *Get back out there.* Don't let your errors keep you from ever taking risks again. Once the mistake is behind you, focus on the future.

40

Identify Your Unique Skills

All of us have at least one disruptive skill—an ability that sets us apart from others. You may have been honing yours for years, or you may be so innately good at it that you don't even notice it. Here are three ways to identify your unique skill:

- *Watch your reflexes.* You may instinctively do what you're good at without even noticing. Ask yourself: when I feel most successful or invigorated, what am I doing?

- *Look for confluences.* A distinct skill may not be one thing, but an unusual intersection of ordinary proficiencies.

- *Listen to compliments.* Peers, managers, direct reports, and even spouses are often good mirrors of your inherent strengths. Don't habitually dismiss compliments, but mine them to discover your unique skills.

Become a Thought Leader

Everyone has a personal brand these days. But if you want to move ahead, you need to be more than the "finance guy who understands the business." Distinguish yourself as someone with a truly unique perspective respected inside and outside the organization. Here are three ways to do that:

- *Build your online presence.* The Internet is a perfect place to start showcasing your knowledge. Post comments on blogs, write your own posts, and connect with other bloggers to create a network.

- *Win some awards.* Identify awards that matter in your industry and don't be afraid to nominate yourself, or convince colleagues to do it for you.

- *Flaunt well-thought-of affiliations.* Your associations aren't always in your control, but if you have a degree from a top school or testimonials from important people, display them prominently. Credibility by proxy is valuable.

Focus on Your Distinctive Skills

When selling yourself in the talent marketplace, focusing on hard-won strengths required for the job in question can be all too easy. These skills are often the ones that many other people have too. Your most outstanding talent is probably something you do without even thinking. Ask colleagues or friends what strengths you might be undervaluing. Lead with these exceptional skills instead. Articulate to prospective employers, or to the boss who's considering your raise, your unique value proposition as an employee. Employers don't just want someone slightly better than everyone else; they are looking for someone with a truly distinctive skill set.

43

Remove Your Mental Barriers

If you have your sights set on the top job at your company, organizational barriers are likely standing in your way. This may be especially true if you are a woman. However, the mental barriers holding you back may be just as strong, if not stronger. To get what you want, you need to ask for it and, in some cases, push for it. Never assume that you are going to be treated fairly or justly rewarded. You must define what you want and present the case for why the company should give it to you. Organizational bias is real, but don't let your own timidity or fear of self-promotion make you lose out on what you deserve.

Sell Yourself—the Right Way

Are whispers about layoffs in your company growing louder? If so, advertising the value you deliver to the organization is more important than ever. But selling yourself is a delicate art. Overdo it or take the wrong approach and you may look like a grandstander.

Sell yourself effectively by describing your contributions to your boss and linking them to important organizational goals. For example, "I put a lot of advance work into that new customer database, so it's really rewarding to see it pay off in greater customer loyalty and profits," or "I worked hard to organize the launch meeting because I really want to see us start major projects off on the right foot."

45

Perfect Your Personal Elevator Pitch

A personal thirty-second story is not just for job seekers. Being able to talk about yourself and your unique talents is a useful skill for building relationships and projecting confidence. Here are three tips for perfecting what to say about yourself:

- *Focus on the relevant, not the recent.* Your most recent job experience shouldn't necessarily be what you talk about first. Think about your audience and lead with your most relevant skills or experience.
- *Focus on skills.* You don't have to have a background in marketing to be good at marketing. Talk about your relevant skills and how your experience is applicable to the situation at hand.

- *Connect the dots.* Your pitch shouldn't sound like a résumé but should tell a cohesive story. Bring together the richness of your experiences and demonstrate how they add up.

46

Develop a Leadership Brand

A leadership brand tells people what is distinctive about you as a leader and communicates what you have to offer. Summarizing your brand in a statement is a useful and often enlightening task. First, answer two important questions:

- What do I want to be known for?
- What results do I want to achieve in the next twelve months?

Take these two answers and put them into the following statement: I want to be known for _____ so that I can deliver _____. Once you have your statement, be sure that you are living up to it. Ask others for input on whether you are achieving your goals and whether they see your leadership brand in the same way you do.

How to Craft the Job You Want

Not engaged and motivated by your job? You may have the power to change it. Begin by identifying your motives, strengths, and passions to help you better understand which aspects of your job will keep you engaged and inspire higher performance. Then, create a diagram of your current job, including your job tasks, noting which you do most often. Next, create a diagram of your preferred job, indicating which things you want to do more or less of and which tasks you want to add. This chart can help you articulate what you want to do differently. Be sure to engage your supervisor in this process; assure her that you won't let your current tasks slide and that any new tasks you propose are central to the company.

48

Ask for a Raise

Asking for a salary increase can be a nerve-racking task. Here are three tips for making the request go smoothly and increasing your chances of getting the raise:

- *Choose the right time.* It's best to discuss a raise when your status is high. Consider asking soon after your team posts good results or at the end of a successful project. Avoid making the request when your boss is preoccupied with other issues.

- *Have a plan.* Know what number you want, make sure it is realistic, and build a case to support it. Use facts about comparable roles and evidence of recent successes.

- *Be clear and positive.* Stay focused on the positive of what you have accomplished. Avoid bringing up other issues during the meeting. Be clear about what you want without issuing an ultimatum.

Control Promotion Anxiety

A promotion can feel both rewarding and stressful. After you've accepted all the congratulations, it's time to deal with all of the new expectations. Here are three tips to address the anxiety that most people feel when stepping into a new role:

- *Prepare support.* Identify a strong ally, mentor, or coach who you can lean on during the first few months on the job. Ask this person to give you honest and constructive feedback along the way.
- *Create a plan.* Lay out what you plan to accomplish in your first few months. Be realistic and set clear priorities so that you are prepared to make necessary trade-offs.
- *Know your limits.* A new job means new responsibilities, but be honest with yourself about what's in your control and what's not.

Become One of Tomorrow's Top Leaders

What qualities and responsibilities will define the most effective leaders of tomorrow? And what skills and knowledge should you attain to become one of those leaders?

- *Change management.* As markets and technologies shift and advance, organizations and strategies must continually change and adapt. The leaders of the future will need to be masters at managing change.

- *Deep familiarity with emerging markets.* Tomorrow's leaders will need to identify and seize the new possibilities created as emerging markets take center stage in the global economy.

- *The ability to inspire and motivate.* In a future marked by constant change, the ability to inspire and motivate others to work together to achieve common goals will be critical. Without alignment, change initiatives stand little chance of success.

- *Lean management.* Leaders will need to operate in—and create—lean, flexible organizations that optimize efficiencies without sacrificing quality.

Managing
Your Team

Become an Inspirational Leader

Leaders need vision, energy, authority, and a natural strategic ability. But those traits won't help you inspire your employees to be their best and commit to you as a leader. Here are the four qualities you need to capture the hearts, minds, and spirits of your people:

- *Humanness.* Nobody wants to work with a perfect leader. Build collaboration and solidarity by revealing your weaknesses.
- *Intuition.* To be most effective, you need to know what's going on without others spelling it out for you. Collect unspoken data from body language and the looks people share across rooms to help you intuit the underlying messages.

- *Tough empathy.* Care deeply about your employees, but accept nothing less than their very best.
- *Uniqueness.* Demonstrate that you are a singular leader by showing your unique qualities to those around you.

Become a Creative Leader

Yesterday's leadership skills will not work in today's fast-moving and evolving world. Only creative leaders who are visionary and empathetic will succeed. Here are five things you can do to succeed as a creative leader:

- Instead of commanding, coach your team and organization toward success.
- Don't manage people; facilitate them. Often, the know-how, experience, and solutions are there; help people to discover them.
- Cultivate respect by giving it, instead of demanding it.
- Know how to manage both success and failure, not just success.
- Be gracious. Be humble about your successes and, whenever possible, give someone else the opportunity to shine.

Lead Confidently

Confidence is a key ingredient in leading effectively. Unfortunately, sometimes it's easier to know your weaknesses than your strengths. Ask yourself these two questions to help find your self-confidence:

- *What do you do well?* Make a list of your strengths. These items are not the same as the accomplishments on your résumé; they are what made those accomplishments possible. How will your strengths lead you to future success?

- *Why should people follow you?* Look at situations where you mobilized yourself and your team to face a particularly tough challenge. Why did people believe in your ability to get things done and trust that you were the one to follow?

Master the Fundamentals

There are countless opinions on how to be an effective leader, but it's important not to forget the basics. Here are five rules for mastering the fundamentals of leadership:

- *Shape the future.* Articulate where your company or division is going and be sure everyone around you understands the direction.
- *Make things happen.* Once you know where you're headed, focus on how. Again, be sure all of your people know what executing will take.
- *Engage today's talent.* Make the most of your people; engage and inspire them to do their best.

- *Build tomorrow's talent.* Find and build the talent you need for future success.
- *Invest in yourself.* You can never be a perfect leader; find ways to continually build your skills and become better.

Keep It Simple

Every generation of leaders thinks it's facing a new set of challenges that require new models of leadership. But being an effective manager is not about mastering mysterious and complicated methods. It's about keeping it simple and following old, proven, and even obvious ideas. What made a good leader in the past is still what makes one today: being competent, caring, and benevolent. Before you discard this old model in exchange for the latest reinvention of management, take a close look at the new method. Often it's the same message in a new package.

06

Avoid the Tendencies of Bad Bosses

Being the boss is hard, especially when you need to counter the natural tendencies that separate you from the people you manage. Recognizing these tendencies can help you avoid them. Here are the top three to watch out for:

- *Self-delusion.* Not only do bosses have this tendency; the majority of people estimate their skills to be higher than they are in reality. Be aware that you might be self-aggrandizing and find ways to get input and evaluations that show you your true skills.

- *Heedlessness.* Those in positions of power are watched carefully by the people below them. But that level of attention is often not reciprocated. When you become the head honcho, don't forget to remain curious about and engaged with your direct reports.

- *Insulation.* No one wants to deliver bad news to the boss, so the boss often doesn't know the full story. Create a culture in which the messenger isn't shot, but is lauded for bringing important information forward.

Don't Be a Martyr

The best bosses shelter their people from disruption and stress. But you shouldn't put your employees' happiness first all the time. Sacrificing yourself will only lead to burnout and resentment. This is especially true if you have weak or destructive people on your team. Whether you hired or inherited them, your job is to help them improve and, if they don't, to help them move on.

Be a Both/And Leader

In today's tough economy, should leaders be dogged, analytic, and organized or should they be empathic, charismatic, and communicative? The answer is simple: they need all those traits. Rather than categorizing yourself as a certain type of leader, explore the nuances that a complex, fast-moving business environment requires. Leaders need to confidently deliver tough messages with analytics as evidence, but they also need to be sensitive to how people receive those messages. Most leadership traits are not an either/or choice, but rather complementary sides of effective management.

Managing Your Team   79

Give Your People What They Need

Traditional leaders see the employee-boss relationship as a transaction: money in exchange for labor. Transformational leaders know and recognize that employees want much more than that. Here are the four things your people need to succeed:

- *Love.* This may sound touchy-feely, but love simply means concern that is focused exclusively for that person's good. Show your employees you care about them and their future.
- *Growth.* No one wants to stay exactly where they are forever. Create a culture that allows your people to grow and expand.
- *Contribution.* To feel fulfilled, employees must know that they are contributing to

the whole. Emphasize the ways that their work matters to the organization.

- *Meaning.* People seek meaning in their work. Share a vision that demonstrates how all of your employees are engaged in a larger purpose.

10

Improve Your Team's Performance

Managing your team's performance is a challenge no matter what the environment. Take the extra time and effort to help your team members succeed:

- *Offer perspective.* Relieve pressure by encouraging them to have fun and remind them work is not the only thing in their lives.
- *Make time.* Devote attention to all your team members, not just the stars. It's easy to focus on A+ performers, but success relies on everyone doing his or her job well.
- *Move on.* When something doesn't go as planned, acknowledge the setback and move on.
- *Focus on team success.* Celebrate what the team has accomplished together, rather than individual achievements.

Support Your People

Countless distractions, threats, and roadblocks prevent people from getting work done. Good bosses take pride in shielding their people from these annoyances. Here are three ways you can help your employees focus on what matters:

- *Show up on time.* One of the biggest detractors from work is wasted time, possibly time your people spend waiting for you to arrive for meetings or give needed direction. Being important doesn't give you permission to impede productivity.

- *Stop the intrusions.* Set aside time for your employees to think and work; don't expect them to respond immediately to voice mail and e-mails.

- *Let them have good fights.* Don't avoid conflict. Make your people feel safe enough to speak their minds, even to you, so they have productive and creative disagreements.

12

Bring Out Their Best

The brightest leaders don't rely on their own intelligence just to succeed, but use it to help their people shine as well. Here are three ways you can help your employees not only feel smarter, but act smarter:

- *Look for ideas everywhere.* Don't assume you know where all the new and creative ideas will come from. Involve people on projects not because of their titles but based on their ability to contribute.

- *Encourage openness.* Create a safe environment where your people know they can—and should—think, act, and speak with reason. Have a high tolerance for mistakes so people aren't afraid to take risks.

- *Challenge people to get better.* Offer opportunities for them to stretch their thinking and behavior. Set the expectation that everyone, including you, should improve his or her skills.

Pat Employees on the Back

An abundance of studies have demonstrated the power of touch on everything from rhesus monkeys to students in a classroom. A pat on the back or a brief touch on the shoulder can express support and reassurance, making the recipient more willing to take risks and improving his decision making. Next time you want to communicate support to a colleague, convey your intention through a small touch. Often times, contact can be more powerful than words. Use touch sparingly though, and don't linger. It only takes a brief moment of contact or a verbal "pat on the back."

Let Your Employees Fail

Good management is somewhere between controlling and ignoring; your job as a manager is to figure out the right balance. When you see an employee making a mistake, you may want to intervene. But people don't learn by being told how to do something right. Stop yourself from interfering. Let your employee make the mistake and then help her adjust to get it right the next time. Of course, you do need to assess the risks and the consequences of failure; if your employee is about to present a flawed report to the CEO, intervene. But when the risks are lower, be prepared to watch and endure more failure than you might be comfortable with.

Make a Mistake or Two

Very few people feel comfortable making mistakes at work. They fear that they will lose the respect of their managers and peers, and that they will tarnish their reputations. Yet mistakes are often the best teachers. Your people won't learn something new if they only do things they know well. Create a mistake-making culture. Encourage your people to take risks. Help them accept their gaffes and share what they've learned from them. Of course, there are times when blunders are too costly. But for those less mission-critical times, ask your people to approach problems not as experts but as learners.

16

Forgive but Don't Forget

Common wisdom holds that failure is inevitable, especially when innovating. If you want people to take risks and try new things, failure must be an option. But few organizations have actually created cultures that accept gaffes. To show your support for failure, encourage your people to make the most of their blunders. Try adopting a "forgive but don't forget" approach. Forgive honest mistakes, but make sure employees learn from past failures so they don't repeat them.

Have Your Employees' Backs

In tough times, people feel more vulnerable, and their senses of safety and confidence can easily evaporate. Never has it been more important to watch out for your employees. A boss who supports her people provides emotional and material relief. Don't assume that your employees know that you'd go above and beyond for them. Clearly tell them that you have their backs. And, since actions always speak louder than words, take every opportunity to demonstrate your unwavering support and avoid creating situations in which it seems everyone is for him- or herself.

Avoid the Unilateral-Thinking Trap

Your employees want to see you take action. But to make smart decisions, you need input. If you're like most managers, you probably seek input from people you know best. That can lead you to gather ideas only from those who share your viewpoints. Result? Unilateral thinking: everyone adopting the same point of view.

Unilateral thinking is good for cheerleading squads, but it'll get your unit into trouble. To avoid this trap, make certain your people feel free (and safe) to voice opinions and ideas contrary to the prevailing thought in your group. Go out of your way to seek alternate approaches to problems—from maverick thinkers and those you don't know as well.

Embrace Diversity Tension

Diversity is a strong asset for a company: differences of ideas, methods, and competencies are advantages for teamwork and problem solving. These differences, however, can also cause stress and strain. Don't try to minimize that tension. Instead, use it as a force for productivity and creativity. Prepare your employees to understand others without judging differences; create an inclusive environment where people feel valued for their skills; and emphasize the complementary skills that diversity brings. Finally, recognize and reward successes that result from diversity. By embracing the tension instead of trying to mitigate it, your team will be able to produce more imaginative and creative results.

20

Develop a Culture of Trust

Leadership should not be a solitary act. Leaders need to surround themselves with people who will challenge their ideas, point out their shortcomings, and tell it like it is. To be an effective manager, you need to ensure that honest opinions and information reach you. Get your people to bother you by bothering them. Open-door policies are well intentioned, but you need to go further. Develop a culture of trust and openness. Show your people that you reward candor and that the more they bother you, the better.

Resolve Conflicts

Working with teams can be a frustrating experience, especially when seemingly straightforward conflict devolves into personal or protracted disputes. Next time your team members start throwing proverbial punches, take these three steps to get them to stop fighting and start working:

- *Intervene early.* The sooner you step in, the better. A simple disagreement can turn into a serious conflict within seconds when emotions are running high.
- *Focus on team norms.* Refer back to something the parties can agree on or, hopefully, already have agreed on. Use team norms to guide behavior and help the parties identify common ground.
- *Create shared agreement.* To reach an accord, have the team members talk it

through. With all parties' cards on the table, facilitate an outcome that is amenable to all. Avoid a lowest-common-denominator solution. Instead, find one that integrates all parties' interests.

Motivate Employees Set in Their Ways

Employees who are slow to react can be frustrating, especially in environments where responding and adapting to change quickly is imperative. However, don't assume these slow pokes are trying to undermine progress or resist change. They may have very good reasons for their response times. Next time you're waiting for someone's input, go talk to him. Explain that you are all under pressure and that you value his response. Ask that he get back to you quickly—within a day or so. He may have a thoughtful rationale for proceeding cautiously, and when he realizes that the matter is in his hands, he may speed things up.

23

Drive Real Change

Getting people to change their behavior can feel like an impossible task. Even when the change is positive, people find it difficult to embrace something new. Here are three ways to approach change to make it more palatable:

- *Focus on joy, not fear.* Fear may seem like a powerful motivator, but it actually can make people freeze. Instead, focus on the positives of the new behavior and the joy people will derive from it.
- *Create the crowd.* Despite our professed love of individuality, people still want to fit in with the crowd. Have someone people respect model the new behavior.
- *Harness momentum.* One bank got customers to change their saving habits by rounding up their debit card purchases and putting the extra in a savings account. Make the new behavior easy to master by integrating it with something people already do.

Assess Behaviors, Not Just Results

When star employees churn out great results, you might be tempted to pat them on the back and ask them to keep doing whatever it is they're doing. However, your job as a manager is to understand the behaviors that drive those results and ensure they are in line with your company's values. Here are two ways to do that:

1. *Give separate ratings for behavior and results.* When you combine the two, you can easily give employees a pass for bad behavior when they're producing positive outcomes. Assessing them separately ensures that you can give fair behavior ratings without obscuring the business results.

2. *Use 360-degree assessments.* These are better at assessing behaviors and their impact on other employees. Use the findings to set behavioral goals that each employee can work toward, such as "treat my team with respect."

Give Better Feedback

Feedback is essential to your development as a professional. So why is it so painful to give and receive? Here are three tips to help you give constructive feedback that works:

1. *Focus on business outcomes.* Explain what the company needs—talent development, sales growth, improved service—and frame your feedback as a way to reach those outcomes.

2. *Give it often.* When feedback is reserved for semiannual reviews, people rarely receive it well. Give feedback regularly. You will be more practiced, and your people will be more accustomed to hearing it.

3. *Be specific.* Identify the specific behavior that a person needs to change. State clearly what you want her to do differently. Use illustrative examples that help the receiver understand exactly what you mean.

26

Don't Just Communicate, Explain

Good communicators know they need to use energy and enthusiasm to persuade their audience. Great communicators know they also need to explain what all the excitement is about. Next time you need to share something important, be sure you convey enthusiasm, but also clearly explain what is at stake and answer the question, "What does it mean?" Lay out what the issue, initiative, or problem is—and be clear about what it isn't. Use metaphors only if they are helpful to your point and share details that support your claims. Then, define what you want people to do by establishing clear expectations. Don't lose or confuse your audience with too many details, though; save those for written communications.

Master the Art of Being Assertive

Overly assertive bosses can be seen as bullying and overbearing. But bosses who tend to hold back may be considered wimps. Good bosses find a balance between the two. This doesn't mean you should try to be assertive all the time. Instead, be prepared to use both approaches in different situations. Your team members may need you to challenge them to accomplish a particularly tough goal. Or you may need to be more passive to let them step up. Be flexible. Use your emotional intelligence to determine when being assertive will be motivating rather than stifling, and laying low will be appropriate rather than discouraging.

28

Create a Mentoring Culture

Encouraging older and younger employees to share knowledge, ideas, and advice makes sense. But old-school, top-down programs in which mentors and protégés are assigned to each other don't work as well as relationships that come about organically.

Help mentors and protégés find each other by starting with specific work needs, when one person can contribute to another's project or goal. This establishes the initial relationship in a comfortable, useful way. Later, if the chemistry between the two proves strong, the relationship may evolve into a broader discussion of career goals and personal aspirations.

29

Empower Your Employees

Successful leaders empower their people to make decisions, share information, and take risks. Here are three ways to get out of your people's way and let them take ownership:

- *Give responsibility and autonomy.* Let those who demonstrate the capacity to handle responsibility take on new levels of accountability and have autonomy for their tasks and resources.
- *Focus on growth.* Create an environment where people have the opportunity to expand their skills and are rewarded for doing so.
- *Don't second-guess.* Unless absolutely necessary, don't doubt the decisions of others. This undermines their confidence and encourages them to hold back when they have ideas.

30

Focus Your People on What They're Best At

Most performance review systems set an ideal image of how an employee should act and then point out how each employee uniquely fails to meet that ideal. We call these failures "development areas" and encourage people to focus their energy on improving them. However, improving on weaknesses takes a tremendous amount of energy. Instead, focus your people on their strengths. Encourage them to do what they are uniquely good at. Most importantly, accept their weaknesses. If someone isn't good at spreadsheets, ask another person to do them instead. If you can't take away that part of his job, help him improve enough so it doesn't hinder his strengths.

Identify Hidden Talents

Finding external talent to fill your company's needs isn't always possible. Nor is it always necessary. By paying attention and asking the right questions, you will likely discover a myriad of hidden talents among your existing employees:

- *Turn a compliment into an interview.*
  When congratulating an employee on a job well done, ask exactly what helped her succeed. By better understanding her process, you may uncover an unseen strength.

- *Ask why employees prefer certain tasks or projects.* Preferences can be a view into someone's talents. An employee might enjoy a project because it involves a product she cares about or because it gave her a chance to design surveys. By learning which, you will possibly uncover talents.

- ***Inquire about dreams.*** Ask your employees what they would do if they had their career to do over again. Peoples' dreams often include an aspect of themselves they don't regularly share.

Use Action Learning

One of your most crucial jobs as a manager is to help develop your direct reports' leadership capabilities. Action learning can help. Through action learning, individuals work through actual business problems and apply lessons learned to new challenges. Here's how it works:

- *Assign* an employee a substantial, important project that is "in plan" and for which failure would have visible consequences.
- *Deliver* some feedback that's relevant to the employee and the context in which she will be learning.
- *Debrief* her on the experience of tackling the project, reviewing with her the results she achieved and how.
- *Articulate* the results' business implications.

- *Help* her transfer the lessons learned to future projects.

The more relevant the challenge and the higher the stakes, the more action learning stretches your employees and the more they learn.

Participate in Their Stories

Motivating employees to higher levels of performance is a challenge for most leaders. Often people are motivated to do things simply because it feeds into the story they tell themselves. For example, your star performer regularly exceeds your expectations because she tells herself that she is the kind of person who impresses others, or a team member triple-checks a document because he is the kind of person who doesn't make mistakes. You can fuel internal motivation by understanding and supporting these stories. First take notice of what kind of person your employee wants to be. Then articulate how what you need done fits into or even enhances that image.

34

Manage Your Smartest People

The people in your organization who have the largest capacity to add value are not necessarily those who have the best titles or the most impressive educations. Also, they may not be the easiest people to manage. Here are three do's and don'ts for leading the smartest people in the room:

- *Do* explain things and persuade them. *Don't* tell them what to do. Smart people don't take a leader's word at face value; they need to understand why you're asking them to do something.
- *Do* use your expertise. *Don't* use your hierarchy. Smart people aren't impressed with titles.
- *Do* tell them what to do. *Don't* tell them how to do it. Smart people enjoy figuring out how to do things and will almost always rise to the challenge.

Leverage Your Best People

Too often managers unintentionally hinder or discourage their star performers. This counterproductive behavior is not ill intended. Often the manager isn't sure how to motivate someone who is exceptionally talented. If you are lucky enough to have such high performers on your team, try these three things to make the most of them:

- *Push them to the next level.* Stretch and challenge stars. Find out what they are good at and what they need to learn, and craft assignments accordingly.
- *Let them shine.* Don't hide your stars. Give them visibility. Let others know what they are doing. When they look good, you do too.
- *Let them go.* Top performers need room to grow. If it makes sense for their development, let them move on.

Give Feedback to High Performers

Don't assume your high performer knows how good she is. Instead, use these three tips to give her the feedback she wants and deserves:

- *Identify development areas.* There may only be a few, and you may need to work hard to identify and articulate them, but help your star understand what she can improve.

- *Show your appreciation.* Failing to say thank you is a simple and common mistake. Your stars need feedback and praise just as much as everyone else.

- *Give feedback often.* Don't wait for review time. High performers thrive off feedback, and your job is to give it frequently.

37

Give the Gift of Time and Space

For the past thirty years, the MacArthur Foundation has awarded "genius grants" to creative achievers to support their pursuit of new ideas. With virtually no restrictions on the money and no obligations required of the recipient, the awards are a vote of confidence in what the recipient is capable of achieving, given the luxury of time. Next time you want a talented employee to pursue a new idea, give out a genius grant of your own. It doesn't need to be money; you can give slack time so that your star has breathing room to explore her idea. Giving these awards not only will result in useful new ideas, but will signal to your people that you value creativity and are willing to invest time and resources in cultivating it.

38

Don't Forget to Manage

The distinction between leading and managing is a subject of ongoing debate. Leading is often characterized as the more glamorous job: leaders guide, influence, and inspire their people, while managers implement ideas and get things done. But leaders who focus exclusively on coming up with big, vague ideas for others to implement can become disconnected from their team or organization. Avoid being a "big-picture only" leader. Make decisions and develop strategies that take into account the real-world constraints of cost and time. Stay involved with the details of implementation. Sure, it's easier to come up with ideas and tell others to make them so, but you also need to roll up your sleeves and understand what those ideas take to become reality.

Inspire Your Team

As a manager, one of your key responsibilities is to inspire your team members—to motivate them to give their best on the job, make difficult changes, and overcome major obstacles. Your communication skills can make or break your ability to provide inspiration.

To sharpen up, practice framing a call to action as a challenge; for example, "We can turn our struggling business unit around." This approach lets your people know that if they want a new and better team, they'll have to work for it. You'll lead the charge, but you need their support. As you present the challenge, communicate a sense of hope that will help your team push through the tough choices necessary to survive and succeed.

40

Engage Your Team

Team meetings are supposed to be collaborative events. If you are doing all the talking and your team members are doing all the listening, something's not right. Here are two ways to revive your team and get them to share their best thinking:

- *Share your ideas sparingly.* You may be tempted to share all of your genius ideas up front. Instead, share one or two suggestions at a time. By limiting your comments, you give others the chance to contribute.

- *Ask lots of questions.* Don't worry about having all of the answers. Ask insightful questions that spark discussion. When people speak up, ask them to clarify their ideas so others can understand.

Trust Your Team

Although skepticism has its merits, trust is crucial to team effectiveness. To cultivate trust among your team members, place your trust in them first. Show them you believe they are competent and capable. Value their contributions by trusting them with increasingly challenging tasks and give them the autonomy they need to shine. Leaders who "test" employees can do serious harm to the overall well-being of the team. Trust is a two-way street, and the sooner you start down your side, the sooner your employees will accelerate down theirs.

42

Give the Right Directions

All too often people work really hard on a project without fully understanding how their efforts contribute to the organization's overall goals. Next time your team isn't sure where it's headed, take these three steps:

- ***Don't assume everyone knows the strategy.*** Don't make the mistake of presuming that just because executives have shared the strategy, your people understand it.
- ***Confirm shared understanding.*** Sketch out a "from-to" chart that shows where your organization is now and where it is headed. Share this with your boss and your team to be sure you are all on the same page.

- *Connect the dots.* With your team, create two lists: one of the major projects, and one of the organization's goals. Draw lines between the two lists. If there are projects that don't line up, consider refocusing or killing them.

Take the Extreme Question Challenge

A leader, especially a smart one, might be tempted to provide her team with all of the answers. However, a smarter leader knows that allowing her team to contribute ideas is not only good for the team, but makes for better results. To counter your tendency to do all of the talking, pick a meeting or conversation and commit to leading it by asking questions. Start by presenting a query that will spark discussion. Ask clarifying questions to dig deeper and better understand the ideas. Then use questions to determine next steps. You might find it difficult to avoid chiming in with a statement or suggestion, but holding your tongue ensures that others will use theirs.

Don't Cry Wolf

If you claim that every project or task is critical, your employees will soon ignore your sense of urgency and do things at their own pace (which is likely too slow for you). If everything is important or urgent, then nothing truly is. Use relativity to convey when a project is really critical to your organization or unit. Be selective about when you apply pressure or claim that something has high impact on your goals. The less often you raise alarm, the more likely your team is to respond how you want it to.

45

Get Rid of Negativity

Every organization, unit, or team has both good and bad. As a boss, is it your job to accentuate the positive or eliminate the negative? You should try to do both, but studies have shown that negative information, experiences, and people have a far deeper impact than positive ones. A better use of your time and energy is to focus on clearing your organization of the negatives as much as you can. This may mean tearing down frustrating obstacles or shielding people from destructive behavior. Grumpiness, laziness, and nastiness are contagious, and by reducing those types of negativity you give your people a better chance of success.

Battle Change Resistance

Any change effort is likely to face a few resisters. Unfortunately, even if these resisters are few and far between, they can quickly erode momentum and stop change in its tracks. Here are four tools to help you get people on board:

- *Cold hard facts.* Use evidence to show that change is necessary and possible. Get your facts from multiple sources and be diligent about details; even a small error can discredit your case for change.
- *Counterarguments.* Know what your opponents are saying, and be prepared to acknowledge their concerns and offer a compelling argument for your case.
- *Big picture.* In the short term, change is uncomfortable. Look at the big picture and

explain why the change is the right thing for the long term.

- *Repetition and pressure.* Stay on message, repeat your best arguments, and apply the necessary pressure to turn around the change-averse people.

Align Employee and Company Priorities

Lucky managers find that their employees' interests naturally align with company priorities. If you're not one of the lucky ones, here are three ways to line up what your employees care about with what your company needs to get done:

- *Know your employees' priorities.* Don't wait for review time. Regularly ask your employees what they personally care most about. As a manager, you need to know what drives them.

- *Communicate company priorities.* Tell employees what the company needs to achieve in the next week, month, and year. Be clear and consistent, and do this often.

- *Align interests to responsibilities.* Now that both agendas are clear, try as much as possible to channel employees' interests into relevant company priorities.

48

Don't Assume People Won't Understand

Strategic decisions can be tough to make, especially in a time of limited resources, but communicating those decisions is often a tougher challenge. One of the most common communication mistakes leaders make is to assume their audience won't grasp the complex reasoning behind a decision. Instead of presuming people won't understand, find ways to explain the details, even to those who may not have the same organizational or financial sophistication as you. If your people don't understand, your job is to find a way to explain it to them. All employees deserve to know where the company is headed and the rationale behind key decisions. They will be happier and more productive when they are clued into and on board with the company strategy.

49

Refocus Your Team on the New Strategy

Most strategic change initiatives fail or at least hit some major bumps along the road. If your team is struggling to adapt to a new strategy, try these three steps to get them back on track:

- *Push decision making down.* If people are told to act differently, they feel like "doers" with little control or power. Let people make choices about how they will contribute to the new strategy.
- *Ask for input.* If your people are stuck, ask them to suggest ways to remove the barriers that are holding them back.
- *Share successes.* No one wants to change if he doesn't think the new strategy will succeed. Whenever you make progress, no matter how small, share it with your team as evidence that the new strategy works.

50

Create a Simple Strategic Principle

Helping employees understand a strategy while simultaneously motivating them to achieve it is a dire challenge for many leaders. Creating and sticking to a pithy, memorable, action-oriented phrase can help. When designed and executed well, a strategic principle gives employees clear direction, while inspiring them to be flexible and take risks. A powerful strategic principle forces trade-offs among competing resources and provides a litmus test for decisions. When faced with a choice, an employee should be able to test her options against the strategic principle to make a decision that lines up with the company's objectives.

Managing
Your Business

01

Assess Your Change Readiness

Leaders need to be on the lookout for what today's quickly changing business landscape means to them and their organizations. Here are three questions to help you face the challenge:

- *Do you see opportunities others don't?* Change breeds opportunity. Don't outcompete your rivals; reinvent the rules of the game by finding new opportunities first.

- *Can your customers live without you?* Customers' options constantly evolve. If your products and services aren't indispensable, customers are likely to move on.

- *Are you learning as fast as the world is changing?* As a leader, you can't afford to stop learning. Seek out ways to evolve and be humble enough to know you don't always have the answer.

02

Create Strategy with Stories

Too often the strategy-creation process produces options that aren't any more interesting or creative than the current strategy. If you find yourself agonizing over which of your carefully crafted strategic options is the right one, chances are you are taking the strategic planning process too seriously. Give up being right and sensible. Instead, tell a story about the future. Make it inspirational and envision your organization in a happy and successful place. Have everyone participating in the process tell his or her own story, and together you'll have created a list of options. Then start the real work of strategy creation: ask yourselves, for these stories to come true, what would have to happen?

Generate Your Next Breakthrough

Business leaders can learn a lot from the way that designers solve problems and create new innovations. Successful designers find new ideas in seemingly mundane places. Here are four steps to finding something original in the ordinary:

1. *Question.* Don't just ask the obvious questions. Look deeper, and don't be afraid to rethink basic fundamentals about your business and products.

2. *Care.* Caring doesn't just mean giving great customer service. Get to know your customers as intimately as possible. Immerse yourself in the lives of the people you are trying to serve.

3. *Connect.* Find ways to bring together concepts, people, and products. Many great breakthroughs are "mash-ups" of existing ideas.

4. ***Commit.*** Give form to your idea as quickly as possible: create a prototype and begin testing it right away. This is the only way to know if you've touched on something truly promising.

Kill More Good Ideas

To come up with a few good ideas, you need to generate a lot of bad ones. And to give your good ideas a chance of reaching their full potential, you need to do some serious pruning. But don't just get rid of the bad ideas; kill some good ones as well. Focusing on many ideas requires thinly spreading your resources. For your truly good ideas to make it to market, they need a concentrated focus and the resources to develop them fully. Make the tough choices and pull the plug on good ideas that aren't quite good enough.

05

Involve Front-Line Employees in Creating Strategy

Even brilliant strategies fail if front-line employees don't execute them well. Many leaders struggle to help their front line understand and buy into new ways of doing things. Next time you change your company's direction, don't relegate strategy creation to a handful of executives. Involve as many of your employees as possible, especially those who interact with your customers. Make them part of the process by bringing them together to think about the company's future. Ask them for input about how the company can achieve its goals. Front-line employees who help make a strategy are far more likely to do a stellar job of executing it.

Survive New Ventures

All new ventures are fragile. Even if revenues are growing (which they should be), chances are your company hasn't yet hit breakeven. To manage through this precarious time, be sure you know these three things:

- *How many days does your venture have to live?* Businesses fail because they run out of cash. Knowing exactly how many months or days you have to live can help you better manage costs and your funding strategy.
- *Why you are doing this?* Success requires hard work and constant attention. If you don't know exactly why you should make the effort, neither will your funders.
- *What are the top-two critical issues?* Be precise about which two issues deserve the highest priority. These may not be the most urgent, but they are the ones that your venture's success depends on.

07

Don't Get Distracted

In business, it's important to set goals—achieve a sales target, grow the company—and lay out the strategies you believe will get you there. A clear strategy that dictates the process for achieving goals can be comforting, but be careful not to let it distract you. Don't keep your head so focused on the process that you lose sight of the bigger picture. Look up every once in a while and remind yourself what you are trying to achieve. Markets change, customers change, and even your company changes; looking up ensures that you don't miss new and important opportunities.

08

Avoid Certain Types of Failure

Innovation experts have long argued that companies should be more tolerant of failure. But not all failure is created equally. Here are three types of failure that rarely contribute to learning and should be avoided whenever possible:

- *Knowingly doing the wrong thing.* When a project falls apart because someone hid information or misled others, any learning is moot. Failure is only acceptable when the project was done with good intentions.

- *Failing to gather the right data.* Often you can avoid failure by doing some simple research: asking target customers for input or testing an idea before launching it.

- *Prioritizing research over experience.*
  Some things are unknowable without real-life experiments. Don't waste resources on researching a theory when you can create a prototype or conduct an experiment that will give you a more realistic answer.

Don't Avoid Risk

Risk management departments are springing up in many companies. They categorize and analyze risk to the company before it happens, and in most cases, they create systems and processes to prevent risks. But the reality is that all hazards can't be predicted or avoided. Instead of simply staving off risk, focus on building resilience so that when the unthinkable happens, you're better prepared to face it. Look at all the risks you face and play out what you would do if any of them were to come to bear. Having systems in place to respond could save you valuable time, money, and resources.

10

Survive Like a Small Business

For every small business that goes belly up, there are dozens more that are thriving. Here are three lessons for how you can operate like a small business to survive even the deepest of downturns:

- *Agility.* Small businesses have a great advantage in a fast-changing world: they adapt quickly. Without layers of bureaucracy slowing them down, they can react quickly to changing circumstances.
- *Rapid testing and refining.* Social media and online marketing tools allow even the smallest of businesses to do real-time market testing. They can also engage customers and build a community around their business.
- *Planning.* Plans are often outdated as soon as they come out of the printer. Small businesses tend to focus more on planning and less on plans. They watch their surroundings and act accordingly.

11

Prepare for a Crisis

You can't prevent all disasters. Companies often face unforeseen or unpredictable circumstances. However, leaders need to ensure their organizations are equipped to stop most crises before they happen. Prevention requires three things:

- *Pattern recognition.* Encourage your people to share information and make connections so that you can recognize when a problem is forming.
- *Broader communication.* Communication across silos is not easy, but it should be mandatory so that critical information reaches all parts of an organization.
- *Trusted leadership.* Leaders need to react quickly when a problem surfaces. Showing that you care about an issue is critical to gaining your employees' trust in your ability to handle problems.

12

Don't Shy Away from a Temporary Solution

When looking to make a change, reorganize a unit, or develop a new system, people often seek solutions that will last as long as possible. They want them to be sustainable. But nothing lasts forever. Finding a permanent solution may be infeasible and even foolhardy. Next time you need to make a big change, come up with a temporary solution—not a final one. Most approaches are useful for a certain length of time. When that time's over, you need a new way to attack the problem, which is likely to morph.

Fail Cheaply

Failures in the innovation process can be costly and time consuming. So why not reduce your failure rate to as close to zero as possible? It's a lofty goal and one that very few innovative companies have ever achieved. Plus, failure is important to innovation—how else do you learn? Rather than eliminating failure, focus on reducing the cost of failure by doing these three things:

- *Make your experiments cheaper.* Experiments need not be expensive. You don't need to recreate a concept exactly to test it. Find low-cost ways to test assumptions.
- *Change the order of experiments.* Test strategic assumptions before logistical ones. Confirm the market need before perfecting a product.

- *Make decisions faster.* Larger organizations often let bad ideas linger. Accelerate decision making when it comes to innovation and get rid of flawed projects before they cost you time and money.

Stretch Your Marketing Dollars

Companies need creativity and resourcefulness to stretch dollars when cutting budgets. Fortunately, doing more with less doesn't necessarily mean reaching fewer customers. Instead of reducing message frequency, consider shifting from TV to less expensive radio advertising. Create different versions of an ad for different markets or segments rather than separate commercials for each. Consider Internet advertising if you haven't before. Because the medium provides immediate feedback about what's working and what's not, now may be the right time to experiment with search or banner advertising.

15

Be Smarter at Cost Cutting

Almost all companies have or will need to cut costs to survive in the current environment. Unfortunately, not all do cost cutting smartly. Consider these three pieces of advice before making cuts:

- *Put strategy first.* Cuts across the board rarely, if ever, lead to effective results. Laying out strategy first helps you decide where to cut and also helps employees accept the cuts as a step toward a goal.

- *Focus on good customers.* Rather than cutting valued services to valuable customers, "fire" high-maintenance customers who create unnecessary complexity. Focus on serving your more cost-effective customers who are happy with your products and services as they are.

- *Keep your business simple.* In a healthy economy, it's easy to overlook processes and activities that are redundant or overly involved. Simplifying them can save you money, with the added bonus of increasing both customer and employee satisfaction.

16

Put Constraints on Innovation

Google has long been the envy of blue-sky thinkers and innovators who admire its world-class and nonbureaucratic approach to innovation. But even Google needs limits. The company has announced it would begin using formal processes to ensure that senior leaders give resources and attention to the right ideas. Don't assume that processes and constraints will inhibit innovation; they often accelerate it by focusing creativity and ensuring that funding finds projects with the highest returns. Create a process to structure and guide innovation. Just be sure that the process doesn't become a burden and squash innovative ideas with unnecessary bureaucracy.

17

Beware of "New and Improved"

Companies love to introduce "new and improved" products. Yet, often these new innovations are useful to the company but not to the customers it aims to serve. For example, a self-checkout lane may help a company reduce the number of cashiers it needs, but may be a hassle for customers who are baffled by the new machines. Before you roll out a new service, feature, or product under the new-and-improved claim, be sure to learn whether it is something customers want. Evaluate new innovations through the lens of the market, not just the lens of your organization.

18

Put the "I" Back In Alliances

Strategic partnerships yield great benefits for those involved, but they are fragile entities. To ensure success, remember these eight I's when forging alliances with other organizations:

- *Individual excellence.* Both sides bring strengths, and neither can be expected to prop up the other.
- *Importance.* The relationship must matter strategically to both sides.
- *Interdependence.* You need to need each other.
- *Investment.* Have a stake in the partner's success.
- *Information.* Transparency strengthens the partnership; hiding information impedes trust.
- *Integration.* Create several points of contact across the organizations.

- *Institutionalization.* A formal structure can aid in objectivity and ensure the partnership works for both sides.
- *Integrity.* Trust is critical and ethics are a must.

19

Build Strong Partnerships

Today's economy is forcing many organizations, both big and small, to consider acquisitions or mergers. Before fully integrating your organization with another, consider forging a strategic alliance that may give you and your partner lower costs, greater scale, or broader market scope without sacrificing independence. For smaller organizations, consider forming alliances to reduce costs of duplicative activities. Nonprofit organizations can partner to market to prospective donors. Regardless of the reasons, proceed cautiously, as alliances can be difficult to build and even more complex to maintain.

20

Think Like a Small Business

Big companies used to win out over small ones because of their experience, impressive client lists, and seeming permanence. We trusted big business because it was big, but the economic crisis has changed that. Small companies are now winning the confidence and the business of customers. No matter the size of your company, restore customer trust by doing what small companies do well:

- *Be available.* Customers of small companies don't need to holler "agent" into a phone to talk to a real person. Make it easy for customers to find you; react quickly to requests and demands.

- *Keep your promises.* Always follow through on what you say you're going to do.

- *Grow and sustain.* Consumer confidence is shaken, and customers want to know that businesses are going to be around no matter what the economic situation. Assure customers you are acting in a financially responsible and sustainable way.

Innovate with Less

Even large corporations need to innovate as start-ups do when resources and time become scarce. Here are four tips for innovating in a tough economy:

- *Forget the big budget.* Innovation doesn't have to cost a lot. Rely on open-source software, online market research tools, and virtual prototypes to test ideas cheaply.
- *Test in the real market.* Don't waste time endlessly perfecting ideas before you launch. Get a "good enough" design out there, then test and refine in the market.
- *Skip the business plan.* Focus on making the idea happen, not planning every detail.
- *Make decisions and move on.* Tough times require quick decision making. Don't be afraid to wind down ideas when they start to fail. You'll free up scarce resources for the next good idea.

Stop Ignoring Growth Opportunities

Chances are that someone inside your organization has a great idea for how to grow your company. Chances are that leadership is ignoring that idea. Kodak long ignored an engineer's idea for a "filmless camera" (aka a digital camera) because it was in the business of selling film. The largest growth opportunities are often the market-changing ideas that represent not only growth but a threat to your business as well. Figure out what those threats are before someone else does. Ask your people: what could put us out of business? In the answer to that question may be your biggest source of innovation.

Answer These Strategy Questions Simultaneously

The two essential strategic questions are: Where should a company play? How can it win there? Answering these requires analysis and logic, but most importantly, creative integration. Many good strategists focus on only one of those questions, trying diligently to figure out how to globalize or deliver a new product. A master strategist addresses both questions simultaneously and ensures the answers fit together. Don't rely on a single logic or analysis, but creatively integrate your company's choices about what market to play in and how to win there. The integration is what sets superb strategies apart from those that go nowhere.

24

Make Small Bets

How can you help your company become an innovation powerhouse? Don't put all of your resources into big bets on possible new offerings or business processes. Instead, conduct many small, inexpensive experiments in safe venues, such as quick pilot projects to test out ideas for a new product or way of serving customers. Use these small experiments to see what's working and not working. Then iterate and refine to produce a successful final innovation.

Amazon did this by conducting experiments—Kindle, Amazon stores, and elastic cloud computing—to identify and capitalize on unique growth opportunities beyond the company's core book business.

Spur Innovation

New challenges require new ways of doing things; this means not only a new approach but a refusal to be bound by the rules that applied in the past. Here are three ways to spur innovation to address your next challenge:

- *Look outside.* When faced with the need to innovate, most companies turn to their inside talent. Instead, reach across corporate boundaries to your extended network.

- *Mobilize passionate individuals.* There are people who are likely passionate about your product, idea, or area of focus. Find those people and connect them so they can share ideas and mobilize one another to innovate.

- *Embrace new technology.* Look to younger generations of employees to see what technologies they are using. Support and embrace these technologies, as they may be the source of your next innovation.

26

Take Baby Steps

Every innovator hopes for and works toward breakthrough innovations. But in tough economic times, innovation often requires too much risk for an organization and its change-resistant customers. Instead of dreaming of "the next big thing," focus on innovating in smaller, shorter bursts. Look for improvements to current products and services. Use small and cheap experiments to test new ideas. Seek out innovations that consumers can easily adapt and don't require huge investments. These innovations are more likely to be palatable to your stakeholders and customers, and they're often the building blocks for larger, longer-term breakthroughs.

Don't Put Out the Fire

Forest fires are an essential part of a healthy ecosystem. They rid the forest of old underbrush that otherwise could serve as fuel for an even larger fire. Recessions are the economy's forest fires; while painful, they seem to be necessary. Rather than compensating for dips in the economy, prepare for them as opportunities to rid your company of excess and develop your organization's resilience. When the fire is out, discover the room you now have for new things to grow—new ideas, new strategies, and new opportunities.

28

Create a Social Platform

More and more companies are introducing social networking tools to help employees connect. However, these should not be considered "work versions" of Facebook or Twitter. These platforms are intended to support your work, not give you a place to post pictures of your poodle. Here are three ways to make good use of these tools to advance your work:

- *Narrate your work.* Talk about your current projects: where you are, what you're struggling with, and what you're producing. This will help others who may be doing similar work find you.
- *Ask questions.* Often, collective wisdom is out there. If you're stuck, ask the crowd to help you out.

- *Talk about social activities.* If your company's softball team won last night's game, post it. Socializing is an important part of work, and these tools are perfect for supporting it. You may want to dedicate a specific part of the platform to socializing, however, so people can avoid it if they want to.

29

Establish Your Relevance

Many companies' forays into social media yield nothing more than wasted time and effort. Before you establish a company Twitter account or start a Facebook page, step back and think about what messages will be relevant to your customers or potential customers. If your brand and your communications aren't useful or interesting to them, you might as well be tweeting into a black hole. Start by understanding the conversations about your brand that are already happening. Then craft messages accordingly. Before sending anything out, ask yourself: What value does this message carry for our customers? What action are we hoping to inspire? If you don't have a sharp answer to these questions, it's time to return to the drawing board.

Invest Wisely in Social Media

30

Invest up front to grow your social ecosystem and regularly feed it new ideas, insights, and content. Whether an internal wiki, a Twitter account, or a blog, all social media initiatives require careful monitoring and management to capture value. Social media that aren't well tended risk lack of adoption and participation, and become anything but social.

31

Tell Your Story

What's your company's story? What makes it unique, and how does it positively affect people's lives? If your company is not getting its story out to customers in a consistent, thorough way, it's losing out on a chance to distinguish itself from rivals. And in today's dire economy, that can be fatal.

Use the latest technology to spread the word. If your company serves businesses, make sure your marketing message can be consumed via Black-Berry. If it serves consumers, be certain to put an application in the Apple App Store. Creating consistent and coordinated touch points will broadcast your company's story most effectively—and engage your customers.

32

Define Your Purpose

Great companies have a single purpose that drives them toward success. That purpose is simple, straightforward, and can be stated in one sentence. For example, Google's is, "We organize the world's information and make it universally accessible and useful." ING Direct's is, "We lead Americans back to savings." Your stated purpose should not be a tagline but a single idea that defines your company's reason for existing. Discover what your company is best at and put it into a sentence. Don't settle for being middle of the road, but strive to be the most responsive, most colorful, or most focused. Then, make sure that everyone in your company knows that sentence and uses it to be successful.

33

Find Your Company's Inner Self

Sometimes the economy forces companies to take a hard look at what they do. Some will need to reinvent themselves to survive. Here are three tips for finding your company's inner self and developing a plan for recovery:

- *Find your company's purpose.* Don't focus too much on spreadsheets and data. Figure out what your company stands for. Most great and adaptable companies have a purpose that is larger than their products.

- *Don't (necessarily) mess with the business model.* Struggling companies often try to revamp their business models. If your customers still have a need for the business you're in, you may only have to recommit to your business model rather than reinvent it.

- *Focus on quality growth.* Companies that grow for the sake of growth rarely survive a downturn. Growth should be driven by quality, not quantity.

34

Don't Control the Customer Experience

Whether or not you're aware of it, every interaction your company has with its customers contributes to their larger experience with your organization. Perhaps your company knows this and carefully and thoughtfully crafts each experience in hopes of influencing opinions. But, despite calculated efforts, customers will not always perceive your company as you wish. People don't behave or react exactly how you expect they will, but don't give up because of this unpredictability. Accept it as part of the challenge and frequently monitor what customers are experiencing. By getting their input and feedback, or better yet, observing them in real time, you can adjust efforts accordingly. Perfect control is not necessary to influence their opinions. Continue to aim for the ideal and modify as needed.

Externalize Your Focus

Organizations that are too inwardly focused often miss important happenings and opportunities in the market. Use these three ways to get your people to look outward for customer insights, competitor moves, and market changes:

- *Listen to customer-facing employees.* Front-line employees are your ear to the pavement. Value them, ask them what they hear from customers, and if necessary, train them to listen for the right information.
- *Get people out.* Send executives on sales calls. Ask directors to train as customer service reps. People calling the shots should meet customers face to face.

- *Share data, both good and bad.* Some executives protect their employees from troublesome market or customer data. While well intentioned, this hinders your organization's responsiveness. If there is bad news, deliver it with a well-articulated plan.

Help Boost Your Company's Online Sales

Disappointed by your company's online sales? You're not alone. The problem isn't that Web consumers are cheap or disloyal. It's that most companies aren't exploiting what online shoppers really want: engagement.

You can engage your firm's Web site visitors by giving them information on products and services related to your core offerings and brand. Porsche, for instance, uses the Web to offer adventure tours and travel information, reinforcing its image of passion and high performance.

Learn what customers are interested in by offering them a list of topics and asking them to vote on their favorites. Use their responses to decide which attributes (wealth, attractiveness, exclusivity) you want customers to associate with your company's brand. Then provide supplementary information that helps them make those associations.

Energize Your Online Customers

Competing for your customers' attention online can be tough, especially when you're up against dancing banner ads and all of the daily e-mails customers get. Here are three tips to cut through the clutter and capture your customers' attention in this crowded space:

- *Create a sense of urgency.* Send out a coupon that needs to be used by midnight or offer a free product to the first fifty respondents.
- *Energize your customers to tell their friends.* Word of mouth is incredibly powerful and valuable, especially on the Internet. Give your customers something exciting that they'll want to share with their friends.
- *Make it fun.* Whatever the interaction is, keep it simple, fresh, and engaging.

Look for Customer Motivation

While knowing how your customers break down into measurable categories is helpful, typical demographics don't tell you much, if anything, about how your customers behave. To truly understand their motivations and ultimately why they do or don't buy your products, ask customers about their purchase experiences. With the purchase as the "end goal," what steps do your customers take to achieve that goal? What is their thought process as they take each step? What obstacles are in their way?

Understanding their answers will help you create and market products that your customers—not their demographic category—truly want.

39

Use Customer Passions to Grow Sales

Have you ever loved a product or service so much that you couldn't wait to tell everyone you know about it? All over the Web, people's passion for products has led them to share their love via YouTube videos, blog posts, and Facebook groups. These "natural" spokespeople have created valuable buzz and initiated sales growth—all for free. Find your most devout customers and encourage them to talk about your products in their online forums. Ask them to rave on their blogs or create Facebook groups in support of your product. Thoroughly search the Web to see if natural spokespeople are already singing your product's praises. If so, harness that passion for free.

Improve Customer Service

Advances in technology and pressure to cut costs have changed the customer service experience. Companies now push far more function and responsibility to the consumer. Here are three ways to support and involve your customers in this new paradigm:

- *Be transparent.* Show your customers your company's internal systems so they feel part of the experience, not separated from it. For example, consider how shipping companies now allow customers to schedule pickups, print labels, and track packages on their own.

- *Convert or capitalize on tribes.* There are groups of people who are going to blog, tweet, and find other ways to praise or complain about your products. Find your company's tribe and make it an ally in delivering a positive message.

- *Open the door to new talent.* Some of your customers may be so enthusiastic about your product that they can sell it better than you can. Find ways to discover who these customers are and capitalize on their talents and passions.

41

Create a Seamless Process

For companies that care about the customer experience (and who doesn't?), integration is a must. Choreograph all your customer touch points so customers have a seamless experience, whether they walk in your store, reach your call center, or use your Web site. Be sure the systems and processes that support this coordination are in sync. Often, companies have channel-specific silos that are culturally and logistically at odds. Create incentives that encourage your people to coordinate across those channels. Look out for those who are barriers to a harmonized customer experience. If they can't learn to coordinate, it may be time for them to make room for their integration-minded colleagues.

Move Beyond Demographics

Traditional demographic information, such as gender and age, is only so useful when getting to know your customers. Psychographic information reveals far more about customers' preferences and purchasing habits. If you understand how your customers interact with the world and what they value most, you are far more likely to be able to give them what they want. Ask them questions geared at their personalities and preferences. Use association-based questions, such as, "If you were a car, what kind of car would you be?" The answers will help you better profile your customers so you understand which products they want and how to market them.

43

Appeal to Their Emotions

The recession created unprecedented consumer anxiety. Consumers don't trust companies to stay around or to do the right thing. This means you need to tap into your customers' emotional sides. First, understand what makes them anxious. That anxiety may be distrust of your product or concern over their family and community. Then, craft a simple, emotional message that directly addresses that anxiety. For example, at a time when many consumers feel financially unstable, one insurance company created a Web site explaining that because it is owned by its policyholders, it's more likely to keep its promises.

Win Their Hearts

Customers are far more likely to purchase a product or service if they feel valued by the person selling it. Underappreciated customers will look elsewhere to make their purchase. Reach out to your customers and make sure they know how important they are to you. Give them the opportunity to meet as many of your staff as possible, all the way up to the CEO. Thank them for their business and ask them to tell you about their company. When you create an emotional connection with them, they are more open to hearing what you have to offer and much more inclined to purchase. The connection needs to be genuine, however; your overtures shouldn't be phony or insincere.

45

Speak Effectively

Successfully communicating with customers is the foundation for all sales. Here are two tactics that will increase the likelihood your customers hear what you have to say:

- *Understand their language.* Too many companies use a one-size-fits-all sales pitch. The reality is that your customers speak a unique language informed by their life experiences. Tailor your approach and your language for each customer.

- *Focus on them, not you.* When trying to make a sale, you might be tempted to talk about "my company, my product's benefits, my product's features." Instead, turn the spotlight on your customers. Talk about their problems, their values, and their purchasing plans.

46

Use Words, Not Numbers

When it comes to customer data, many believe that multiple-choice surveys across large samples that can be statistically analyzed yield the most rigorous research. This type of analysis, however, only gives you a shallow understanding of your customers. To get more nuanced information, use qualitative methods to discover what your customers think about your products and services. Qualitative techniques, such as focus groups or open-ended questionnaires, let you delve deeper into the relationship between your firm and those who buy or use your products. They also allow your customers to express their opinions using their own words, not yours.

Handle Customer Complaints

All organizations depend on customer feedback to make their businesses better and increase customer satisfaction. Yet customer complaints take up an inordinate amount of time and money, and the complainer doesn't often get what he wants. Here are three tips for expediting the complaint process and keeping customers happy:

- *Understand the full context.* Try to understand as much as you can about the complaint. The more information you have, the easier it is to determine the root of the dissatisfaction.
- *Propose a resolution.* Know what would make the situation better for your customer and propose ways you can solve the problem.

- *Show respect.* Complaining customers are often upset. Train employees receiving complaints to be empathetic and to reframe the harsh criticism they may receive into constructive feedback.

48

Involve Customers in Product Creation

The best way to get your customers excited by your product or service is to involve them in creating it. Instead of offering them what you think they need, ask them to help you design what they want. If you are a consultant, design the project *with* your clients, not for them. Leverage their deep knowledge about the company culture and personality. If you are in the business of selling products, hold an online contest to bring customer design ideas to the table. Customers who have a stake in the development process are far more likely to feel pride of ownership and be happy with the end product.

Develop Services Your Customers Want

Creating services that captivate consumers and generate profits is tough—thanks to the abundance of offerings, vendors, and channels. (Consider the options available for someone who wants to see a movie.)

To stand above the crowd, don't start with technology. You'll risk creating services that are too far ahead of customers' priorities, too cumbersome for people to use, or too expensive to produce profitably.

Instead, begin with customers' needs—both those they're aware of and those they don't know they have. To uncover these needs, host interactive online forums with sophisticated users who can illuminate what other users may want to do in the coming years. Analyze leading-edge consumer activities in international markets. Take time to research product investments being made in industries related to your service offering.

Simplify

Today's consumers reward simplicity. They want direct connection and streamlined design. Find unnecessary complexity in your organization: Is it in your product offerings, your processes, your services, or all of the above? Do you offer too many product variations? (GM has forty-seven brands of cars.) Or do you have costly functions that need to be better integrated? (Seagate Technology had the highest R&D costs in the industry after accumulating and not integrating acquisitions.) Find ways to cut the clutter in your business. Serve your customers how they want to be served—simply.

Attributions

Management Tips was adapted from the following blog posts and products. Search for them on hbr.org:

Managing Yourself

1. "3 Steps Toward Being a Better Leader in 2009" by Stew Friedman
2. "Choose the Fantasy World You Live In" by Peter Bregman
3. "Top Ten Ways to Find Joy at Work" by Rosabeth Moss Kanter
4. "A Freelancer's Recipe for Professional Development" by Steven DeMaio
5. "Never Let Your Ego Stop You from Learning" by John Baldoni
6. "The Power of Preventive Assessment" by Stew Friedman
7. "Five Questions Every Mentor Must Ask" by Anthony Tjan
8. "Do You Have an Excessive Need to Be Yourself?" by Marshall Goldsmith

9. "Critique Me, Please" by John Maeda
10. "Is Listening an Endangered Skill?" by Bronwyn Fryer
11. "A New Year's Resolution: Schedule Regular Meetings with Yourself" by Gill Corkindale
12. *HBR's 10 Must Reads on Managing Yourself*, one of six HBR article collections in the popular 10 Must Reads series
13. "The Supreme Killer App: Your Memory" by Steven DeMaio
14. "The Next Big Idea in Management: The 3 x 5 Card" by Alan M. Webber
15. "Academia vs. Industry: The Difference Is in the Punctuation Marks" by John Maeda
16. "Burned Out? Take a Creative Sabbatical" by Gina Trapani
17. "Six Ways to Supercharge Your Productivity" by Tony Schwartz
18. "Why Wise Leaders Don't Know Too Much" by Jeff Stibel
19. "Add an Hour to Your Day" by Ron Ashkenas
20. "How to Manage People in 15 Minutes a Day" by Daisy Wademan Dowling
21. "Six Ways to Supercharge Your Productivity" by Tony Schwartz
22. "The Art of the Self-Imposed Deadline" by Steven DeMaio
23. "To Multitask Effectively, Focus on Value, Not Volume" by Ron Ashkenas

24. "Why You Need to Fail" by Peter Bregman

25. *What's Next, Gen X?: Keeping Up, Moving Ahead, and Getting the Career You Want* by Tammy Erickson

26. "Are You the Bottleneck in Your Organization?" by Brett Martin and Thanos Papadimitriou

27. "Are You Micromanaging Yourself?" by Steven DeMaio

28. "Three Ways to Beat Burnout" by Christopher Gergen and Gregg Vanourek

29. "Use Stress to Your Advantage," by Peter Bregman

30. "How to Make Knowledge Work Fun" by Larry Stybel

31. "Grownups Need Recess, Too" by Stew Friedman

32. "Why Do Most Entrepreneurs Fail to Scale?" by Anthony Tjan

33. "Don't Give Up on Change" by Marshall Goldsmith

34. "Why You Should Fire Yourself" by Ron Ashkenas

35. "How Your Brain Connects the Future to the Past" by Jeff Brown and Mark Fenske

36. "How (and When) to Motivate Yourself" by Peter Bregman

37. "A Great Boss Is Confident, But Not Really Sure" by Robert I. Sutton

38. "You've Made a Mistake. Now What?" by Amy Gallo

39. "How to Identify Your Disruptive Skills" by Whitney Johnson

40. "How to Become a Thought Leader in Six Steps" by Dorie Clark

41. "To Get Paid What You're Worth, Know Your Disruptive Skills" by Whitney Johnson

42. "Overcoming the Mental Barriers to Equal Pay" by Mary Davis Holt

43. "Improve in the Delicate Art of Self-Promotion," Christina Bielaszka-DuVernay

44. "3 Ways to Pitch Yourself in 30 Seconds" by Jodi Glickman Brown

45. "Define Your Personal Leadership Brand in Five Steps" by Norm Smallwood

46. "Turn the Job You Have into the Job You Want" by Amy Wrzesniewski, Justin M. Berg, and Jane E. Dutton

47. "How to Get the Pay Raise You Want" by Gill Corkindale

48. "Should You Write Your Own Promotion Plan?" by David Silverman

49. "Don't Let Promotion Anxiety Derail Your Career" by Gill Corkindale

50. "Who Is the Leader of the Future?" Vineet Nayar

Managing Your Team

1. *HBR's 10 Must Reads on Leadership*

2. "Why Are Creative Leaders So Rare?" by Navi Radjou

3. "To Lead More Effectively, Increase Your Self-Confidence" by John Baldoni

4. "Decoding Leadership" by Norm Smallwood

5. "What Every New Generation of Bosses Has to Learn" by Robert I. Sutton

6. "Some Bosses Live in a Fool's Paradise" by Robert I. Sutton

7. "The Boss as Human Shield" by Robert I. Sutton

8. "The Age of the Both/And CEO" by Jeff Kehoe

9. "Four Things Employees Need from Leaders" by Cleve Stevens

10. "Four Ways to Improve Your Team's Performance" by Daisy Wademan Dowling

11. "The Boss as Human Shield" by Robert I. Sutton

12. "Bringing Out the Best in Your People" by Liz Wiseman and Greg McKeown

13. "An Effective (and Underused) Way to Reassure and Motivate" by Peter Bregman

14. "When Should You Let an Employee Make a Mistake?" by Peter Bregman

15. "The Miracle of Making Mistakes" by Vineet Nayar

16. "Forgive and Remember: How a Good Boss Responds to Mistakes" by Robert I. Sutton

17. "Do You Have Their Backs? Or Just Your Own?" by Robert I. Sutton

18. "When the Going Gets Tough, Act the Part" by John Baldoni

19. "Learn to Embrace the Tension of Diversity" by Marshall Goldsmith

20. "Avoid Mistakes That Plague New Leaders: An Interview with Warren Bennis" by Christina Bielaszka-DuVernay

21. "Get Your Team to Stop Fighting and Start Working" by Amy Gallo

22. "Ask the Expert" on the HBR Answer Exchange by Peter Cappelli

23. "How to Drive Change the IDEO Way" by Andrew Winston

24. "Embedding Sustainability/Ethics into Performance Reviews" on the "Ask the Expert: Marc Effron, Miriam Ort" board of the HBR Answer Exchange

25. "Feedback That Works" by Cynthia M. Phoel

26. "Great Communicators Are Great Explainers" by John Baldoni

27. "The Delicate Art of Being Perfectly Assertive" by Robert I. Sutton

28. "Give a Gift: 4 Tips for More Effective Mentoring" by Tammy Erickson

29. "Empowering Your Employees to Empower Themselves" by Marshall Goldsmith

30. "Stop Worrying about Your Weaknesses" by Peter Bregman

31. "How to Identify Your Employees' Hidden Talents" by Steven DeMaio

32. Action Learning: A Recipe for Success" by Chris Cappy

33. "A Story About Motivation" by Peter Bregman

34. "Leading Clever People" by Gareth Jones

35. "Leverage Your Top Talent Before You Lose It" by Ron Ashkenas

36. "Giving a High Performer Productive Feedback" by Amy Gallo
37. "Award Your Own Genius Grants" by Julia Kirby
38. "True Leaders Are Also Managers" by Robert I. Sutton
39. "How to Communicate Like Barack Obama" by John Baldoni
40. "Bringing Out the Best in Your People" by Liz Wiseman and Greg McKeown
41. "6 Questions to Help You Build Trust on Your Team" by Lieutenant Colonel Diane Ryan
42. "How Leaders Create the Context for Strategy Execution" by Ron Ashkenas
43. "Bringing Out the Best in Your People" by Liz Wiseman and Greg McKeown
44. "Vanquish the Time-Management Villain" by Luca Baiguini
45. "Bad Is Stronger Than Good: Evidence-Based Advice For Bosses" by Robert I. Sutton
46. "Four Tools For Defeating Denial" by Rosabeth Moss Kanter
47. "How to Align Employee and Company Interests" by Anthony Tjan
48. "Seven Communication Mistakes Managers Make" by Steven Robbins
49. "When Your Team Reverts to the Old Strategy" by Amy Gallo
50. *HBR's 10 Must Reads on Strategy*

Managing Your Business

1. "The 10 Questions Every Change Agent Must Answer" by Bill Taylor
2. "Moving from Strategic Planning to Storytelling" by Roger Martin
3. "The Four Phases of Design Thinking" by Warren Berger
4. "If You're the Boss, Start Killing More Good Ideas" by Robert I. Sutton
5. "Making Your Strategy Work on the Front-Line" by Amy Gallo
6. "Three Questions for Entrepreneurs" by Scott Anthony
7. "Don't Get Distracted by Your Plan" by Peter Bregman
8. "When Failure Is Intolerable" by Scott Anthony
9. "The Benefits of Thinking the Unthinkable" by Rita McGrath
10. "How Small Businesses Win Big in Tough Economies" by Jeff Stibel
11. "Finding Northwest Flight 253's Lessons for Leaders" by Rosabeth Moss Kanter
12. "Why the Best Solutions Are Always Temporary Ones" by Peter Bregman
13. "3 Ways to Fail Cheap" by Scott Anthony
14. "How CMOs Should Function in a Recession," by John Quelch
15. "A Better Way to Cut Costs," by Rita McGrath

16. "Google Grows Up" by Scott Anthony
17. "Better Through Whose Eyes?" by Scott Anthony
18. "How to Strike Effective Alliances and Partnerships" by Rosabeth Moss Kanter
19. "How to Strike Effective Alliances and Partnerships" by Rosabeth Moss Kanter
20. "Why Small Companies Will Win in This Economy" by Peter Bregman
21. "Four Lessons from Y-Combinator's Fresh Approach to Innovation" by Scott Anthony
22. "Have You Already Killed Your Next Big Thing?" by Mark W. Johnson
23. "Why Most CEOs Are Bad at Strategy" by Roger Martin
24. "Innovate Like Chris Rock" by Peter Sims
25. "Four Ways to Spur Innovation at Your Company" by John Hagel III, John Seely Brown, and Lang Davison
26. "Find the 15-Minute Competitive Advantage" by Rosabeth Moss Kanter
27. "Surviving a Recession—And a Wildfire" by Adam Werbach
28. "Do's and Don'ts for Your Work's Social Platforms" by Andrew McAfee
29. "Social Media's Critical Path: Relevance to Resonance to Significance" by Brian Solis
30. "Debunking Social Media Myths" by David Armano
31. "How Would Walt Disney Market in 2009?" by John Sviokla

32. "What's Your Company's Sentence?" by Bill Taylor

33. "What McDonald's Can Teach Us about Recovery" by Mats Lederhausen

34. "Understanding Customer Experience" by Adam Richardson

35. "Four Ways to Increase the Urgency Needed for Change" by John Kotter

36. "In E-Commerce, More Is More," by Andreas B. Eisengerich and Tobias Kretschmer, *Harvard Business Review*, March 2008

37. "Groupon's Four Keys to Customer Interaction" by John Sviokla

38. "It's Not Who Your Customers Are, It's How They Behave," by Peter Merholz

39. "Looking to Grow Sales on the Cheap? Use Natural Spokespeople" by John Sviokla

40. "Better Customer Service Through Transparency, Tribes, and Talent" by John Sviokla

41. "How Integrated Are Your Customer Experiences?" by Peter Merholz

42. "Want to Understand Your Customers? Go Pyscho" by Anthony Tjan

43. "Are You Catering to your Customers' Anxieties?" by John Sviokla, Anand Rao, and Jamie Yoder

44. "To Win the Sale, Win Your Customer's Heart" by Clif Reichard

45. "Persuasion Tactics of Effective Salespeople" by Steve W. Martin

46. "The Secret to Meaningful Customer Relationships" by Roger Martin

47. "How (Not) to Complain" by John Quelch

48. "The Farm-to-Table Secret to Motivating People" by Peter Bregman

49. "Developing Services Consumers Want" by John Senior

50. "Simplicity: The Next Big Thing" by Rosabeth Moss Kanter

Index

action learning, 107–108
advertising budget, 147
affiliations, displaying
    key, 54
agility, in adapting to
    change, 142
alliances, 152–154
assertiveness, 101
autonomy, importance
    of, 5, 103
awards, 53

behavior
    assessment of employee,
        97–98
    changing your own bad
        behaviors, 10
behavioral change,
    43–44, 96
big picture, focusing on, 35

bosses. *See also* leaders
    assertive, 101
    avoiding tendencies of
        bad, 76–77
    relationship between
        employees and, 80–81
brain performance, 46–47
brand, leadership, 60
breaks
    mental, 19
    mini, 40
    regular, 14
burnout, preventing,
    14–15, 37
business goals, 138
business models, 170–171

calendar, managing
    your, 23
challenges, 43

change
   readiness for, 131
   resistance to, 123–124
   roadblocks to, 43–44
change management, 64,
   95, 96, 127
communication skills,
   100, 115, 186
company priorities,
   aligning with
   employee
   interests, 125
company purpose,
   defining 169, 170
company story,
   communicating to
   customers, 168
confidence, acting with,
   4, 50, 72
conflict, 83
conflict resolution, 93–94
constructive criticism, 11
contacts, making new, 25
contribution, of
   employees, 80–81
control
   delegating, 41
   giving up, 33–34
cost cutting, 148–149, 157

coworkers, enjoying, 39
creative leadership, 71
creativity, 18, 19, 113
credibility, 54
crisis, preparing for, 143
critical thinking, 18
criticism, being open to, 11
crossword puzzles, as
   mental break, 40
culture of trust, 92
customer complaints,
   188–189
customer experience
   creating a seamless, 182
   monitoring, 172
customers
   communicating with,
   186
   demographics, going
   beyond traditional,
   183
   emotions of, 184
   focusing on good, 148
   involving, in product
   creation, 190
   motivation of, 178
   needs of, 191–192
   online, 175–177
   passionate, 179

psychographic information on, 183
reaching out to, 185
trust of, 155–156
customer service, 180–181
customer surveys, 187

decision making, 20–22, 33, 50, 127, 146, 157
decisions
    clinging to, 50
    communicating, 126
    second guessing, 35, 38, 49, 103
delegation, 37, 41
demographics, customer, 183
disaster preparedness, 143
distractions, 43–44, 83, 138
diverse opinions, importance of, 21, 90
diversity, valuing, 91

efficiency, 28
elevator pitch. *See* personal elevator pitch
e-mail, scheduling time for, 37
emerging markets, 64

empathy, importance of, for leaders, 70
employee-boss relationships, 80–81
employees
    assessment of, 97–98
    bringing out the best in, 84
    developing, 34
    empowering, 103
    frontline, 173
    giving feedback to, 99
    hidden talents of, 105–106
    involving in strategy creation, 136
    letting employees fail, 86
    mistakes by, 86, 87
    motivating, 95, 109
    patting on back, as expression of support, 85
    priorities of, 125
    sacrificing yourself for, 78
    supporting your, 83, 89
empowerment, of employees, 103

energy management, 14–15
exercise, 40
expectations, establishing, 100
external focus, 173–174

failure. *See also* mistakes
  accepting, 88
  avoiding, 139–140
  learning from, 30
  reducing cost of, 145–146
feedback, 11, 23, 99, 112
"Fire yourself," as a means of self-evaluation, 45
front-line employees, 173

genius grants, 113
goals, short-term, 31–32
goal setting, 138
growth
  company, 171
  employee, 80, 103
  taking responsibility for your own, 6
growth mind-set, 30
growth opportunities, 158

heedlessness, as tendency of bad bosses, 76–77
hidden talents, 105–106
high performers. *See* star performers

ideas
  capturing good, 17
  encouraging new, 113
  finding new, 133–134
  generating, 135
  getting rid of bad, 135
  implementing, 114
  questioning, 18
image, developing your professional, 31–32
information analysis, 22
innovations, 133–134, 150, 151, 157, 160–162
inspirational leadership, 69–70, 115
insulation, as tendency of bad bosses, 77
internet advertising, 147
interruptions, reducing, 14
intuition, 69

job crafting, 61
job satisfaction, 5

leaders
  qualities needed by effective, 64–65
  thought, 53–54
  traits needed by effective, 79
  transformational, 80–81
leadership
  assessment of, 8
  brand, developing your own, 60
  confident, 72
  creative, 71
  fundamentals of, 73–74
  inspirational, 69–70, 115
  versus management, 114
  simple model of, 75
leadership vision, creating your, 3
lean management, 65
learning
  action, 107–108
  desire for, 7
  growth mind-set for, 30
  from mistakes, 86, 87, 88
listening skills, 12

love, expressed as concern for employee well-being, 80
loyalty, 42

management
  versus leadership, 114
  lean, 65
  of smart people, 110
  of star performers, 111
  team, 82, 93–94, 115, 117
  time for, 24–25
marketing budget, 147
marketing message, broadcasting your, 168
market testing, 142, 157
meaning, as necessity to employee success, 81
meetings, with self, 13
memory, 16, 46
mental barriers, 56
mental breaks, 19
mentors, 102
micromanaging, 33, 35–36, 38
mini breaks, 40
minority viewpoints, 21

mistakes
  accepting, 33, 88
  by employees, 86, 87
  learning from, 86, 87, 88
  recovering from, 51
  tolerance for, 84
motivation, 95, 109, 115, 178
multitasking, 29

negativity, 122
new ventures, 137

online customers, 175–177
online presence, 53
online sales, 175–176
openness, importance of, in developing a culture of trust, 92
organizational bias, 56
organizational goals, 118–119
overthinking, 4
ownership
  importance of, in self-improvement, 43
  as key to job satisfaction, 5

partnerships, 152–154
patience, 43
performance review, of self, 6
persistence, 41
personal elevator pitch, perfecting your, 58–59
pilot projects, 160
planning, importance of, 142
positive outlook, 14
prioritization, 29, 125
proactive brain, 46–47
problem solving, 22, 39
product creation, involving customers in, 190
productivity, increasing, 26–28
professional development, taking responsibility for own, 6
promotion anxiety, 63
psychographic information about customers, value of, 183

punctuality, 83
purpose, defining your, 169, 170

questions
asking, 120
strategic, 159

raise, asking for, 62
recessions, as means of discovering new opportunities, 163
responsibility
employee, 103
for own personal growth, 6
results, focus on, (combined with critical thinking approach), 18
risk avoidance, 141

second guessing, 35, 38, 49, 103
self-delusion, 76
self-improvement, 6–10, 12
self-promotion, 57–59
services, 191–192

short-term goals, 31–32
simplicity, as key to customer satisfaction, 193
skills
focusing on distinctive, 55
unique, 52, 70
small businesses, 142, 155–156
smart people, managing, 110
social media, 142, 164–167, 179
star performers
giving feedback to, 112
managing, 111
strategic change, 127
strategic decisions, 126
strategic partnerships, 152–154
strategic principle, importance of, to employees, 128
strategic questions, 159
strategy creation, 132, 136

strengths
  double-edged, 41–42
  focusing on, 55, 104
  identifying, 72
  reliance on, 9, 31
stress management, 38
success, 48

tasks, prioritizing, 29
teams
  conflict resolution in,
    93–94
  engaging your, 116
  improving performance
    of, 82
  motivating, 115
  refocusing, 127
  trusting your, 117
technology, embracing
  new, 161
technology dependence, 16
temporary solutions,
  advantages of, 144
thought leaders, 53–54
360-degree assessments, 98

time management, 23–25
to-do lists, 26, 28
top talent, 111, 112
touch, power of, 85
transformational leaders,
  80–81
tribes (of customers), as
  business allies,
  180–181
trust, 92, 117

unilateral thinking, 90
unique skills, 52, 55, 70
urgency, appropriate use
  of, 121

weaknesses
  employees', 104
  working on your, 9
Web site visitors,
  engaging, 175–176
work, making it fun, 39
worrying, ways to
  counteract, 4